AF434424

More True Tales of Ghosts and Weird Encounters

S. L. Vadimsky and C. L. Vadimsky

Salt 'n' Pepper Books - Carolingian Press

With Thanks

We thank our family, friends, colleagues, neighbors, and our readers, for sharing their experiences with us, and supporting our endeavors, especially Adriane, Barbara, Brian, Donna, Elizabeth, Jennifer, Jim, John, Mary, Mike, Richard, Susan, Teresa, Tom, Toni, and Thomas's mother; and The Ghosts of Somerville.

We also acknowledge with respect any beings from another time or place encountered here.

Contents

There either is or is not, that's the way things are. The colour of the day. The way it felt to be a child. The saltwater on your sunburnt legs. Sometimes the water is yellow, sometimes it's red. But what colour it may be in memory, depends on the day. I'm not going to tell you the story the way it happened. I'm going to tell it the way I remember it.

Charles Dickens

?

Manhattan Smith

I BOUGHT AN OLD house, built in the year 1800. It is in a very old, historic town, the setting for one of the first railroad lines and one of the first photographers. The area dates back a hundred years before the town was even named Milford. It is on a river, which really floods when the rains are of historic levels. The house was built long before the mills were built on the river, the grist mill, and the paper mill. One of the first railroad lines runs through here, even when there was little else but farms around but our house.

I moved into this lovely old home with my wife and infant son, and our daughter was born and joined our family in this house. Not long after we moved in, we all started to notice peculiar things happening.

Because we were out in the country, we were not too worried about people coming to the house, but to alert us in just in case someone did enter, we hung a string of bells on the back door.

Well those bells started ringing without any cause. No one was at the door, and the bells would be ringing. This would happen periodically throughout the day, every day. The bells swinging back and forth so often made a groove in the door. That was the first bizarre incident we noticed, but gradually we experienced more disturbances.

When my family were alone in the house, we would sometimes hear footsteps walking across the attic over our heads. The footsteps would stop in the middle, right over our heads, and then continue to the other wall. Sometimes it seemed to miss a step, like it was dragging a foot or shuffling a few steps, and then continue walking.

We weren't the only ones to experience weird things here. The house was the perfect location for big outdoor parties, and we would host events like birthdays and holidays there. But many of our guests noticed a strange phenomenon. When someone entered the house alone to use the bathroom, the door handle would jiggle like someone was trying the lock or trying to enter. Our guest would call out, "Occupied!" but the jiggling would not stop. When they opened the door in irritation, they found no one there at all. No one, anywhere in the house. But they all noted the creepy feeling they experienced at that moment.

One thing I had loved about the house was its thick stone walls. I am a drummer, and I use a studio in the basement for playing and for recording tracks. Once when I was working down there alone, I was suddenly conscious that a light had been turned off in the corner. I looked up, and realized that there had never been a lamp or any lighting in that corner. So what light suddenly went out? I realized then, I had been accompanied by some kind of presence of light while I was working, and only realized it once it was extinguished! I stared into the dark corner, where we had no light fixtures at all, and wondered about the light which had been in the room.

Another time when I was down there drumming, recording tracks, about two in the morning, there was a sudden great flash of overhead light which flickered on and off. It was brighter than ordinary incandescent light, it was like a bluish, electrical light. I thought perhaps my family was flashing the light as a signal to me, so I went upstairs to check. Everyone was asleep and the house was dark.

The next morning, they all confirmed they had not been up flicking the light switch.

When I went back later to check the drumming tracks I had recorded that night, there was a voice over the recording! I could distinctly hear a man's voice say, "Noisy!" I had intentionally recorded no vocals, and had heard nothing while I was making the recording. But it was there, every time I played it back. Many of my friends have listened to this recording with me and confirmed what I heard. "Noisy!"

The haunt was making itself more and more obvious.

My children have actually seen an apparition. As a baby, my son's eyes used to track something moving through the room, something invisible to us. This child remains nonverbal. But as soon as my daughter was old enough to talk, she said she saw a man in the house.

Now I figure, if this house is haunted, he was here before me, so I don't have ill will toward this spirit, and we don't really feel any ill will from him. We don't feel threatened. I felt more like he was trying to get our attention. I would occasionally talk to him and say, "just don't scare the children, and we can coexist."

I decided I had to find out more about my house. I was in town doing errands and at one stop, the woman working there chatted with me. When she found out where I lived, she said she used to babysit a little girl in my house, before we lived there. I mentioned I was investigating its history. This woman, too, said she had seen and heard things in the house, during her babysitting there, and had finally been too frightened to return.

I asked what she had seen and decided to test her, to see if she was just making up a story for my benefit. So I asked her about the ghost of a lady.

She looked very confused. "No, there was no lady," she responded, "I saw a man. Definitely a man."

So I did my research. I joined the local historical society. I read the archived documents in the library. I learned that in October of 1877, there had been a terrible train accident. A storm had washed out the stone arch bridge, but the tracks still hung there in the dark. With one lone headlight on the locomotive, the engineer couldn't see the problem in the torrential rain and darkness. The train crashed into the raging river and eight people died. I found a list with the names of seven of the eight casualties. One name stood out to me because it was unusual: Manhattan Smith. He was listed as injured, but it seemed the body had not been recovered to know for certain his end. Bodies had been washed away by the river, one of them found many miles south.

I wondered if, perhaps, one man had dragged himself out of the river, seen a light and come to my house. Perhaps he died here at my house. I figured I had learned as much as I could, and my investigation was complete.

Just as I was thinking this in my kitchen, the lid of a pot flew off the top of the refrigerator at my head and fell to the floor at my feet, dented. I took this as a sign that the situation was not resolved.

As it happens, someone who was also investigating the train accident contacted me through the historical society. She was a great-great-granddaughter of the very Manhattan Smith injured in the accident. They were doing genealogical research incident to administration of an estate.

The house Manhattan Smith had lived in, in Trenton, still existed and was currently for sale. His place of death was recorded as a drowning in Milford. His descendant was curious as to how he ended up dying in Milford, when he lived some distance away in Trenton, and their family was upstate New York. She discovered that he had been in the Milford train wreck.

We learned that he was working for his father's business in upstate New York, where they made pipe. He was commuting home to Trenton on the train, when the October wreck occurred. Manhattan Smith was 28 years old at the time, and was headed home to a wife, two daughters and a third on the way. This great-granddaughter was a descendant of that baby he had never met.

The woman had a strong feeling that she wanted to commemorate him in some way, so she came out to the house with flowers. We went together to the river nearby, the scene of the accident, and she strew the flowers onto the water, with very moving remarks assuring her ancestor that she was OK, that the child he had not known, her line, had flourished, and that they would remember him.

Then friends of mine came to smudge the house. We explained to the spirit that we were not trying to banish him, but that he could move on now, his family was safe and he could pass.

We have not since had any more unusual experiences in the house. I don't know if all is quiet as a result of the family ceremony, or the smudging ceremony. I don't know if our haunting was indeed by this Manhattan Smith, but the way our investigation concluded seemed to bring peace to all.

? UFOs Over Pennsylvania

Christmas Visit

WE ARE FROM NEW Jersey, but sold our house and moved to Pennsylvania when the children were young. I had always loved hunting and all kinds of outdoor recreation. As soon as the chance presented itself, I transferred from my job at the Bell Labs NJ locations, (I had worked in Murray Hill and then Holmdel) to Allentown, Pennsylvania. We sold our New Jersey house in the woods and bought substantial acreage in the heart of farmland Pennsylvania. It is mostly a kind of mountain, very steep land. Our driveway crosses a bridge and winds up and sharply around the top of this steep hill, and is labeled on the maps as a lane with our family name. We built a ranch house on the top of this mount, and a barn and gardens to feed the family. We had a couple horses and pigs and chickens. We all like to engineer things from scratch, and we passed these skills on to the kids, building structures and canoes, butchering our food from the wild or growing it. From our home in this agricultural area, I could also establish a hunting camp way up in the wilds.

When my children were young, we would go back to New Jersey to spend Christmas Eve with the family. On this one Christmas Eve, we traveled back and got home around 11:00 at night, with very light snow falling, and no wind at all. My youngest was about 10 years old. The kids went right to bed and I packed it in probably about a half hour later.

Our window faced east from the house. We went to bed with the drapes pulled back, and the shade all the way up. All the better to welcome the Christmas Day sunrise!

Soon after I fell asleep, I was awakened by a very bright light shining through the window. The light was really extremely bright, and was coming through the window at about a 10-degree angle downward. I could see the light on the closet door on the far side of the room. The light was flashing on and off.

I jumped out of bed and ran around it towards the window. Each time the light flashed, the angle got steeper and steeper, seeming as if the object was rising up over the house. When I got to the window, the light angle was almost vertical, coming through the window and shining directly on the floor. With the next white flash of light, the object was indeed over the house, because I could see the peak of the roof's shadow on the ground below me.

Then with one brilliant red flash of light, it was gone.

I was thinking, perhaps, was it a snow plow coming down the road with a red flasher light on? Then I thought no, that couldn't be, because the shadow was cast on the ground from a light above the house.

I ran out of the bedroom, down the hall and out the front door to stand on the front porch. At that time, before the trees grew up, our whole front field was just an open, sloping farm field. I could see to the west about a mile and to the east about half a mile. There was absolutely no noise, no snow plow. The snow was coming straight down with no wind and everything was dead still.

I went back into the house, wiped my feet off and headed back to bed. I lay in bed for quite a while thinking about what I had just seen. I questioned myself. Could this really have happened? Was I dreaming?

The next morning was Christmas Day, and the kids were up early, so I also got up. As I left the bedroom, my daughter right away asked me, "Dad! Did you see that bright light shining through the bedroom window last night?" Oh, my! It wasn't a dream, it really happened!

About two weeks later, she and I were standing in the open area between the dining room and living room, (the floor plan was open, no walls here). We were just talking. I had my back to the rear windows, and she was standing where she could see out. Suddenly we saw bright white light coming through the rear windows, so I turned around to take a look. The back field behind the house, on the neighbor's farm, went up slightly to a higher elevation. Behind the hill, we could see the same flashing white light. Then from behind the hill, we saw a red flash of light that rose now above the hill, and suddenly, it was gone. Same as the Christmas Eve occurrence, except this time, it was behind the house.

We both saw it. I could not explain what it was, but it surely was not an aircraft.

UFOs Over the Swimming Pool

One summer a few years later, I was out by the pool doing a swim after dark. I was hosting guests, adults and teens. It was perhaps 9:30 to 10:00 P.M., so of course it got chilly once you were wet from swimming. We would always light a fire in the fire pit to warm up after we came out of the pool. There were at least half a dozen people sitting around the fire, could be more, I don't recall how many of the kids' friends were present.

We were sitting around the fire facing towards the direction west. As we sat there, we noticed to the west, low on the horizon, quite a number of white lights in the sky coming towards us.

At the time I thought they were military helicopters, as I've seen those in the daytime, perhaps coming from Fort Indiantown Gap, going towards New Jersey.

As we sat there, we quieted down and started listening to see if we could hear the sound of the helicopters. There were a large number, perhaps 25, 30, or 40. I wasn't quite sure, as there were very many. As they flew, they weren't in a perfectly straight line. They were like bobbing up and down a little bit as they came closer and closer.

As we watched, they started to go up into the sky. They made a cross formation, like a crucifix shaped cross. The vertical line of the cross was perhaps 20 to 25 of these white dots. The horizontal cross was closer to the top and was perhaps 20 more dots.

They stayed in that position for a few seconds, and then all the dots moved toward the intersection of the vertical and horizontal parts of the cross. As they came together, they made a fairly large white ball. Then, immediately, they went vertical, very fast. The ball was visible for perhaps just two or three seconds and then was gone out of sight!

The sky was crystal clear. There were no clouds. We were amazed how the ball disappeared so suddenly. We all sat around talking about what we had just seen. A UFO, or many? We were never sure what we had seen.

?

My Father's College Visit

I AM THE YOUNGEST of three daughters. My dad had been sick for a while but was still working for a long time. His hobby was working on the team of a race car. As a result he traveled throughout the country sometimes, for races. He lived simply while traveling, sleeping in the car in simple pullover rest stop parking. He especially loved Pennsylvania for some reason. He was under the impression people were nicer there, life was simpler and cheaper.

My sisters and I were each of us very close to him in our own ways. When we were born, he had anointed us each with a private nickname which only he used for us. He had still been here for my oldest sister's home wedding. He had been at all my middle sister's track meets. When she became devoted to running, he had learned all about the sport and became her personal coach and biggest fan. He traveled to all her meets. He had seen her off to college and through it, and continued to cheer her marathon running. He himself had never attended college.

I was my parents' surprise baby, a few years after my sisters' times. While my sisters sometimes had their sibling disputes, as the baby, I was usually able to get along with everyone. As I grew up I was especially close to both my parents, as my sisters became older and more involved in activities outside the home with their peers.

I was devastated as we all were by father's death too young. He had become sicker and sicker, couldn't work and was limited to his recliner chair in the living room, with my mother's care. But his death was still a shock when it came. Some people might think that with a long illness, you have some notice of the impending loss, and it is less of a shock. Actually, it can happen that you acclimate to a loved one's illness, that you take them for granted even though they are ill. Because they seem to survive for so very long in the diseased state, it feels very much the same as the life we all lead, a long, very slow dying. They've beat the illness for so long, you don't think it is going to happen any time soon, and you will still have time. So they fade into the background of your everyday routine. You forget.

And then you blame yourself for forgetting, because now they are quite suddenly gone, and you've missed your chance to comfort them, and tell them you love them.

So we were all sharing the misery of our grief. And I had to grow up and go to college and get married, without my father.

When it was time, I chose to attend a college in Pennsylvania. I had a good time there. I joined a sorority and met lifelong friends. I met my husband there. One year, my sorority sisters and I decided on an apartment off campus. I would have my own room.

We came back to school that September and moved in. It was our first night in the new place, and I was feeling a little lonely and strange in my new bedroom. I got into bed and was sitting up in the dark, gazing across the room at a window, and noting the way the sky glowed from streetlights in town.

Suddenly a shadow crossed the room, blotting out the window light for a moment. I saw and felt an impression sinking into the mattress at the foot of my bed, and shifting the covers a bit from my feet. I didn't feel frightened, though. I should have been scared during this experience, the first night in a strange old apartment. I should have been afraid that we'd moved into a haunted house.

But as I sat there with someone in the dark, with someone invisible except for his weight near my feet, I just felt warm, and loved. I just knew it was my father visiting me. I felt his approval. I listened, in hope of hearing his pet name for me, but there was no sound. I felt as cozy and content as if he were hugging me. While he sat with me, I felt safe enough to fall asleep, with a smile. It was just as if I'd been a little girl again, and he sat with me in my room during night terrors, until I fell asleep.

In the morning, everything was normal. I wondered what it was that had happened. None of my roommates had had any strange experiences, and I never had this visitor again. I have to believe that it was a visit to me from my father.

Now I feel that I can bear the loss a little, with faith that somehow he knows what I am doing in my life, and sees his grandchildren now. I believe that we will meet again.

?

No Doubt

I T WAS LATE FALL or early winter. I drove to the Siskiyou mountains in Southern Oregon to visit friends for a week or so. It's a full day's drive, so by the time I arrived I had just enough energy for a hearty reunion dinner with my friends, lots of laughing, a quick clean-up, and then the walk up the dark trail to the cabin where I always stayed when I visited.

Not too far off the main path to the common house, and up a wooded hillside a bit, stood this tiny cob cabin that backed up against thousands of acres of sparsely inhabited land. The cabin was fairly secluded and hadn't been occupied for many months. Blackberry bushes reached into the path and madrone trees seemed to have grown like weeds around the perimeter of the cabin since I'd last visited.

I walked up the familiar dirt path to the front door, remembering all of the wonderful times I'd had in this cozy cabin. All of them alone. Some of them had been a time for hibernating and healing. Other weeks or months had been a fresh start full of creativity and enthusiasm. I opened the door and sighed.

Because it was now dropping into the low 40's at night, I brought in a few armfuls of firewood from the wood shed, before I even unpacked my pack.

Once the fire was roaring, I closed the dampers halfway and organized my clothes and food, before climbing the steep stairs to the loft where the featherbed awaited. The cabin was fairly airtight so there weren't too many signs of mice, although a fair number of spiders had set up shop in most corners.

It didn't take long for the place to warm up, being just under 200 square feet. I went back down the steep steps, damped down the stove, brushed my teeth, and then headed back up to the loft for a deep sleep under a thick down comforter.

After a restful night's sleep, the early morning chill woke me before sunrise. I tossed and turned trying to ignore the cold. Finally I braved the brisk air and went downstairs to stoke the coals. A couple split logs did nicely to bring the fire back to life. Though it was still dark, the sky was clear. The light of the nearly full moon bounced off a dusting of snow that had fallen the day before.

Once the fire was going strong, I put the kettle on the propane stove to heat up water for coffee. I loved to "rough" it, especially when there was rich, strong coffee on the shelf! While the kettle rumbled, I put on layers of wool and my coat in anticipation of my most sacred ritual of the day: morning coffee outside. Whatever time of year, whatever the weather, being outside with the air on my face was the best start of a day I knew.

Soon enough, with my coffee mug in hand, I went out the back door which opened onto a small deck about ten feet square. Beyond the deck, there was a patch of grass and young madrone trees that went uphill for about 30 feet to the edge of a thicker, older forest which was a mix of conifers and hardwoods.

I took two or three steps out the door with my coffee mug against my lips and froze. I heard steps. Like a person's steps, crunching in the leaves and coming toward me from my right and up the hill. Crunch! Crunch! Crunch! My brain went into overdrive trying to quickly make sense of it. Was it the neighbor?

But his house is way down the gulch. And it's so early in the morning. Who would be walking this way so early?

A few seconds later, an upright, dark figure on two legs appeared right in front of me. The creature was just up the hill, barely in the woods where the taller trees started. He, or she, turned his head and looked right at me. He stopped. Just for a second. Then continued walking. He took two or three more steps.

Then everything went quiet. No more crunching. He was just gone. I didn't actually see him disappear, but I didn't hear another step.

I stood there in shock with my coffee mug still against my lips, replaying it all in my mind. It was still pretty dark, but there had been enough light from the moon reflecting off the snow that I'd been able to see his hair. It was black, with dark gray streaks. I couldn't tell how long it was. I remember I could see its texture. His or her build was bigger than an average man's, maybe six and a half or seven feet tall.

I quickly retreated into the cabin where I spent the next few hours trying to calm down.

Later that morning I joined my friends down at the common house for breakfast. I could hardly wait to share what had happened a few hours earlier. I had seen a Sasquatch! What else could it have been?

My friends didn't know what to make of it. They weren't sure if they believed me that it was a Sasquatch, but they said they'd heard of other sightings in the area.

I have shared this story with some people over the years and never once cared if they believed me or not. It's one of those experiences in life where you just know what you saw. No doubt about it. I heard what I heard and saw what I saw. A big, hairy animal walking on two legs like a human.

The following year I visited these same friends, but during the summer instead. I took a walk on a fairly overgrown trail that headed past this same cabin and continued along their property line. About 200 feet from the cabin a well-traveled game trail crossed the trail I was on. The trail seemed to head down the hill toward the cabin. Exactly at this intersection was a young sapling about two to three inches in diameter that was broken at a ninety-degree angle about five feet off the ground. It was as if someone had just snapped it like a twig. It looked to be a fresh break. The inner wood was moist and yellowish.

I'd read that many people have also come upon these snapped saplings too big for a human to break. Some think it's evidence of the Sasquatch marking their territory as a warning to humans to stay away. Who knows?

Others say that the Sasquatch People are interdimensional. That they are able to quickly "disappear." Sometimes Human People who have found Sasquatch tracks in the snow say that the tracks simply stop. They go nowhere.

Where's "nowhere?"

?

Sightings Over the Experimental Farm

W E LIVE IN A rural bedroom community within commuting distance of a densely populated city. By bedroom community, I mean there really isn't employment or shopping within the borders of our town; there isn't even a high school. People are bused to school or work elsewhere, or drive, or take the train. Most people work at one of many pharmaceutical companies in the surrounding area, or do finance work in the city. Our town is filled with residential housing now, even though it used to be farms. There are no working farms left, only some Christmas tree farms for the tax benefit. There are a few local chickens to make omelets for families on all-protein diets, on their way to fitness training elsewhere. We hear one rooster at all hours.

Well, there is one local place, which calls itself a farm. There's a fenced, gated area on River Road, where there is no housing development. It's mostly woods, but up a great hill there are cleared fields. A small, formal white sign with fancy letters hangs on the fence gate, and it bears the brand name of a plush toy stuffed animal, and the words "Experimental Farm". Or maybe it is a pharmaceutical brand? There are no buildings, and I've never seen animals there. Not farm animals. I am not counting the deer, which are everywhere here in herds. I have seen a white deer in the woods by this Experimental Farm. That is interesting, but I supposed an albino deer is possible in nature. I have never seen a white deer anywhere else.

When we were kids, there was one animal which had escaped from there, and rampaged through our street. It was a monster bull, 10 feet high. Its feet left holes in our front lawn almost two feet in diameter. And our soil here is not soft mud, but hard clay. A fleet of State police cars had to come to herd it away. (We didn't have local police in our town, either.) That is my brother's story, I hadn't remembered it.

Anyway, River Road is a pleasant drive, high, narrow, cut through above the river and the train tracks, and below a steep bank of houses. It is swervy, hilly and dark. Not too dark, because the flood plain across the river is parkland,

and lit for much of the night, until it's really late. That park is behind some riverbank trees, and has a ball field but mostly dirt rings for horse shows. The lights just make a pleasant general glow in the sky, you can't really see them through the trees.

River Road is our route home, because we live on the hill between the two highways which take people to their errands and workplaces. River Road connects the highways to our little neighborhood of small, older single-family houses, the first ones built on a farm subdivided and long gone.

As a young adult driving home late from work or social events, I always relaxed on reaching River Road, smoothly floating not too fast up and down its hills, coasting home at last. Looking at the river sparkling in moonlight. Checking the Experimental Farm. Nothing there. Just some gutters under the gate pointing at the road and the river. Sometimes a pair of weird reflecting animal eyes skittered by, low to the ground, possum, raccoon. I might get a little tense to see animals scurrying across the road in my headlights, I didn't want to hit them, but usually what looked like mice turned out to be leaves blowing, and I would breathe, and relax. Almost home.

That is, the drive used to be relaxing, until one night, when I was followed. There were no other cars on the road, and I was just motoring gently along. I was in the dip of the road by the Experimental Farm gates. Suddenly a bright white light shone through the rear window, blinding me in the mirrors. I hadn't seen any flashing emergency lights or headlights behind me, the floodlight was just suddenly there. I didn't know what to do. I wondered if I should pull over, in case it was a police stop. But I was on a dark and lonely road. I think the law says I can proceed to the next public parking lot to pull over? I kept driving, not too fast, the limit in this dip in the road was 25 mph. Was it someone high-beaming me to drive faster, or make room for him to pass? If it was the police, I didn't want to speed...The light seemed so bright I felt like I would be sunburned or something.

As I started up the next hill, the light behind me rose up over my car, and went out. Just disappeared. There was no traffic at all but my car, all the way home.

I didn't really figure it out. It was a weird thing. I didn't know what it was that happened. But I don't usually worry about explaining such things. I just assume, well, who knows what happened. There is probably some explanation. I didn't stop driving on River Road.

Over the years, this same phenomenon happened to me maybe twice again, in the same place. The next times it wasn't right behind me, shining through my car. The next time, I saw it coming up behind me, getting closer and larger and growing brighter, then it rose up behind me out of my field of vision until it was over my car. And once I actually saw it pass overhead very fast, going upward until it disappeared. Nothing like plane lights flying and getting lost in the clouds. And this was long before the possibility of drones or something would come to mind, as I was young then. I am old now.

Then my grown son had an experience in the same spot. My son is an educated technology science professional who was working in the finance industry in the city. He is not easily fooled. He very confidently dismisses most mysterious tech tales, and typically, (in tongue-in-cheek use of the parlance), accuses the eyewitness of "user error". He hadn't known anything about what I had seen there.

He just came home one day and told us he had seen a UFO. He had been commuting home from work. He was on River Road in front of the Experimental Farm. There were no other cars, or helicopters, or planes. Just a dark, quiet night. Suddenly a bright spotlight shown next to his car, on the passenger side. It traveled along the road with his car at the same speed, keeping up next to his car. Just as suddenly, the light extinguished, before the field turned to woods. There was nothing to see or hear in the sky or anywhere about. He remains unsettled by this unexplainable event.

Not too long ago, I saw something originating in this spot, but I saw it from a different perspective. I was driving in the evening on the highway, heading for a grocery store, amidst plenty of traffic. I saw something in the sky, in the direction that would have been over River Road. A great ball of light hung in the North. I have an amateur interest in astronomy, and I am always conscious of the sun, moon, planets and constellations on display on a given evening.

This was neither the setting sun nor rising moon, though it was larger than the largest super moon illusion. It hung quivering for moments as if we were driving right into it, and then it shrunk, rose higher and finally winked out. It was nothing like the fireworks from that site on the 4th of July, nor like any marketing beam.

Nothing happened with the traffic all around me. People proceeded to their stores and restaurants. I don't know if anyone else remarked on it. We just went about our business, as we do. Don't know what, nothing to be done about it.

?

Old Dutch

Insider – Tom

THE OLD DUTCH PARSONAGE was built in 1751. It served as the residence of the parson of three local congregations of the Dutch Reformed Church. Rev. Frelinghuysen and his family lived there, and he tutored young men seminarians there. The next parson was one of those seminarians, Rev. Hardenbergh. The house served as a parsonage until 1810, when a local doctor bought it and used it as his family's home.

In modern times, the place is a historic site, not only for its age, but because of the Frelinghuysen and Hardenbergh names, the first two parsons, whose families were prominent in local Revolutionary War history, and because Rev. Hardenbergh was a founder and the first president of Queen's College, now known as Rutgers.

For many years, the association supporting the house's preservation employed custodians to offer tours to the public. I was in charge back in the 1970s. The place had already long had the reputation of being haunted, but I was a skeptic.

Many of our women guests said they felt frightened or ill at ease upon entering the house. People swore they heard footsteps on the second floor. Even though I didn't believe in ghosts, I played along. One of those ghost hunter types pleaded with me to let him investigate the house by bringing in a psychic. So I agreed. I didn't see any harm in it, and thought I would find it kind of funny.

Psychic

I was asked to see what I could find out about a potential haunting in the Old Dutch Parsonage, a beautiful historic building. When I entered, I immediately felt the presence. I spent a good bit of time upstairs where people had made observations. I touched the walls and opened myself to communication from the spirits.

The house was most certainly still occupied by someone who had lived within the house, but not at its beginning. The house already had a long history of habitation by the time this spirit lived in it, in the 19th century. I learned that he was male. It came to me that he was a young man, very young. He worked there; he had been the youngest male servant. Something was deeply bothering him. The thing was something which might appear trivial to others, but his grievance was important to him. I felt he had some issue with women. I began to see the letter M, associated with a woman who made him angry. M was to blame. She was making him move. He wasn't ready to leave his room. She made him change rooms. She forced this upon him and he wasn't ready for the change.

I didn't understand anything else about this transaction. Perhaps it was a moment in time I witnessed. Maybe in his youth, he didn't have understanding of this woman's reasons. Maybe at that moment in time, he did not yet have understanding of anything that would happen later, as a result of the change. Or maybe something more had happened. I felt only his deep disturbance over being made to leave his room.

The energy was very strong in one corner of the second floor room.

Insider – Jim

I am a historic preservationist specializing in the Georgian period, which is the architectural period of this house. I have education, training and work experience in a number of historic sites, including in Virginia and New Jersey. I retired from my professional position at the Old Dutch Parsonage after 32 years of showcasing its history for the public on tours, and otherwise participating in custodianship of this historic gem.

When I came on board, the house already had a convincing history of unusual phenomena. The Parsonage is said to be haunted.

A prior caretaker of the house, Tom, had passed the psychic's story on. I find the letter M intriguing. From 1810-1836, the house was inhabited by a Dr. Peter Stryker and his family and servants. The name of Dr. Stryker's first wife was Maria Mercer. His second wife was named Mary Magdalena.

Law Enforcement

I was a law enforcement ranger. In New Jersey we have Park Police, who have full law enforcement authority, as do US Park Rangers. Both jurisdictions administer not only parks within our jurisdiction, but historic sites.

Back in the 1970s, the superintendent of the Old Dutch Parsonage and I were in the house on a day when it was closed to the public. We were there to check on a malfunctioning oil burning furnace in the cellar.

While inside, we had the exterior closed and locked. But when we were downstairs at the furnace, we both noticed that it sounded like someone was in the building. We heard someone walking around upstairs, and then walking down the stairs.

We went up to investigate. The door remained locked. No one appeared to be in the house. Then we heard the footsteps again, walking on the second floor. "Hello?" No response.

"We're closed!"

"No one should be in here! Come down now!"

"Show yourself now!

I started up the stairs, but then I stopped. We heard footsteps start down the stairs. I put my hand, ready, to my weapon. I fixed my eyes on the stairs, on full alert. The footsteps continued down the stairs. Suddenly they stopped, at the landing right in front me.

The superintendent and I stared at each other. We had each heard this. But saw nothing.

We investigated the house entirely, and found no one.

I will admit that I remained fearful of that house. It is hard to know what to do on a call to a house with an invisible, nonliving trespasser.

Contractor

I work for an alarm contractor. I was contacted by the proprietor of the Old Dutch to do some work installing wires in the garret. Jim arranged with me to come in to do the work on a day they were closed. It was his day off, but he would come in, to let me in to do the work.

He let me in and locked the door, since the building was not open to the public that day. He showed me where to do the work, and I got started.

He then said he was going to get some takeout for lunch. He offered to pick up something for me, and I thanked him but declined, as I was on a limited diet. I thought I heard him leave.

A little while later, while I was working with the wires, I heard him walking around on the second floor.

I called out, "Jim? That you?" No answer. I still heard the footsteps. "Hey! Jim! Stop messing with me!" No response. "Jim?" I was getting irritated, let me tell you.

I slammed down my tools and went to look downstairs. No one was there.

I went back to work with vigor, figuring the guy was being a jerk, stomping around downstairs and then hiding from me. I felt like I wanted to get out of there.

But then I heard the door open and slam, and Jim started up the stairs to find me. I scolded him.

"What d'you think you're doing? Why'd you ignore me?"

"What? I told you I was going out to lunch. What do you mean?"

"I heard you walking around. Why didn't you answer me when I spoke to you?"

Then Jim said, "Ah, I get it." He explained to me about the second floor footsteps people hear in the house, and that it might be a haunting.

I tell you, that got my attention. I looked around at everything with a fresh perspective. And I quickly finished up and got out of there as fast as I could.

Girl and her Mother

My daughter was about five years old. It was a very hot summer day. Looking for something different to do, I decided to go see our local historic sites, the Wallace House, a temporary home for George Washington and his family during the Revolutionary War, and the neighboring Dutch Parsonage.

My daughter and I concluded our tour of the Wallace House without incident, and then came over with our historian host, Jim, to the Parsonage. No one else was around. Jim said it was slow in the summer. They tended to have more visitors during the school year, when more people were around in town.

We climbed the stairs with our tour guide, to the second floor. When we entered one room up there, my daughter absolutely freaked out. She screamed she wanted to get out of here. I removed her from the room. Once in the hall passage, she was immediately relieved and calmed down.

When we got outside the house, I explained to Jim that my daughter was sensitive. Neither of us wanted to use any "ghost" word in front of the child, so we spoke very generally, implying rather than specifying what we were talking about. He asked, does she often—? I nodded, noting that wherever we go, if there is any "history of—" she is certain to pick up on it. Jim nodded. When my girl was out of earshot, he said that some visitors had noted their observations of spectral activity.

Not long after this visit, when we were home baking cookies for something to do, my daughter started talking about the Dutch Parsonage. She said that upstairs in that room she had seen a "man-boy". She said he was angry, and sad, and that is why she was so frightened.

Later I called and informed Jim of what she had said, so he would have the information for the history of the house.

Pastor

I am a Lutheran pastor. My son was to be married, and the women were attending a bridal shower locally. So my son and a friend of mine accompanied me to visit the Old Dutch Parsonage. My son knew the preservationist, Jim, who gave tours of the site. I had never visited there. We thought it was an engaging way to kill the time, on a historic tour of the house and grounds.

When we climbed the stairs I started shivering with cold. Then we entered a room and I felt overwhelmed.

"Does anything—'funny'—ever happen in this room?" I asked.

"Why, are you feeling something?" Jim responded.

"Oh, yes!"

Jim led me to one corner of the room. "What do you feel here?"

"Much—stronger—", I managed. I was feeling darkness, and a very strong malevolence. It was an evil feeling.

Jim led me out into another room to discuss it. He told us that that corner where the darkness felt strongest, was where a little girl visitor had freaked out.

I nodded. I turned to my friend. "Remember the one we cleaned out, down the shore, last year?" He nodded solemnly.

Jim said, "What? Are you telling me you do this? You can 'clean out' hauntings?"

I turned to him and offered to get rid of the thing, if we could, with prayer. I recommended we try. I had the feeling the thing was malevolent, demonic perhaps.

So we went back into that awful room. I offered my prayers. After some time I felt stronger and stronger with God's aid and guidance, and the darkness diminished.

"That's it," I said. "It's gone."

I hadn't imagined we'd be dispelling evil spirits while the bride-to-be was celebrating with our womenfolk, but I'm humbled and grateful that I responded to the call.

Outside

I grew up in town. When I was younger, sometimes my friends used to get together and hang out on summer evenings in the yard behind the Old Dutch, when it was closed. We gathered there just as a place to be together away from parents, to talk and party.

The house itself was dark, but it has large windows on both sides, and there's a streetlight on the road in front of the house, so there's some ambient light coming through. Then periodically there might be headlights from cars turning onto the street. The street is not a throughway, but still, people live there and occasionally come and go. So these lights shine right through the house and move on.

Inside the house, we would see the black shadow of a very tall man, walking through the house on the second floor.

? Haunted Library

I WANTED TO "RETIRE" from the stressors in my professional career and return to working with children, as I had been a teacher when my children were younger. I found what must surely be everyone's dream job, as a Children's Librarian. It is virtually impossible to switch into work as a librarian later in one's career. Most libraries require a Masters Degree in some form of Library Science, or what is commonly now known as Information Science, given the reliance on technology in today's libraries.

However, I had found an independent little old library which time seemed to have forgotten. While most neighborhood libraries had since become mere branches of a merger with the huge county library system, this one remained independent. Some patrons even proudly described it as a rebel. This library had succeeded in remaining independent because of the loyalty and support of the local citizens, who loved the charm and homeyness of the historic site. It also hosts memorial artifacts in remembrance of a local military hero killed in the Second World War.

I was invited to interview. My appreciation for the history of the building, my teacher certification qualifications and good references got me into a job as the Children's Librarian. I assume that's how I got in. It's possible they were just desperate, as library work usually includes night and weekend hours, and this position was framed as a temporary one, a leave replacement. That suited me, since I was exploring job changes.

Now this library was really, really old, from the perspective of American architecture at least. The area had been settled by Dutch colonists, pre-Revolutionary War. The land itself had been "purchased" for next to nothing from the indigenous people living here. The west wing, now the Children's Room of the library, was the original and oldest part of the building. It is reported that it was originally probably used as a tavern, public meeting house and jail. Now it felt cozy and charming. The ceiling had thick, dark wood beams, and wood planks, unplastered. You stepped down into this large dark room filled with rows of bookshelves. A huge old brick cooking fireplace made up the entire rear west wall of the room.

The other rooms were added on later, with some materials imported from Holland. The windows throughout had that ancient thick wavery glass, except those random panes which had had to be replaced with modern glass. There were at least three fireplaces in the building. There was a center hall staircase, dividing the main house. On the left were the adult reading rooms. The reading tables were long dining tables and Windsor chairs, and the room was lined with books and armchairs. Over each fireplace were period paintings of the Mr. and the Mrs. of the house. He had an enormous drooping mustache and those eyes which watch you wherever you are.

The family who made it into a beautiful Federal style home were a prominent area family, officers in the Revolutionary War. I thought it interesting that in modern times, one of the descendants of this family purchased the house from an interceding owner who was renting it out as apartments. As it was being restored to its historic glory, intended for family occupancy, the owner quite suddenly donated the building to the town, within the year. I always wondered why.

In the renovations, one of the later wing additions to the house had been knocked down. Since use as a library, a large new meeting room was added for media events, and a new back stairway had been added, linking the second story with the basement. That was a staff only back stairway, and was not accessible from the public rooms except as an emergency exit.

As I was getting used to my post in the children's room, I occasionally noticed a distinct stink of cigarette smoke. I would walk around the library and try to find the source. Oddly enough it smelled strongest in a spot exactly in front of my large teacher desk. Now of course smoking was prohibited in the library, and though I investigated, I never found any smoker or evidence of smoking anywhere in the library, except for this occasional stink in this exact spot. When I smelled it, I even went to the windows or the door to check outside. Sometimes people would gather on a sunny day on the corner, to play an online search game. Nothing, no one. I was even a little embarassed by the odor, I was afraid someone would accuse me, the Children's Librarian, of sneaking a smoke.

And then there was the classic haunted library occurrence: a book would fly off the shelf. Of course I assumed it was just, I don't know, gravity? That a book had been precariously placed and finally toppled. But every time I checked, there was no such problem. In fact, I might carefully replace the book on the shelf, and return to whatever I had been doing, and a book would fly off again. It wasn't always the same book; these were children's picture books, and I don't remember one in particular. But it was in the same general place in the library, one row between the first two shelves near the door. And it would happen when I was alone in the room, in the midmorning after story hours concluded, or in the evening when I was doing reshelving throughout the room. I would hear the thump, and find the book on the floor. I would never find a book on the floor when I entered the room from having been somewhere else.

Then there was the new, back staircase added to the East wing. That part of the house gave one a very odd feeling. Perhaps it was just because it didn't fit in with the rest as to historic period. But even though the staircase was well lit by frosted skylight windows as well as electric sconces and emergency lighting, it always felt dark and lonely and silent. And it felt oddly cold, even windy, somehow. We used to keep things on those back steps to keep them cold. Winter or summer, it was always cold there. It wasn't just because the heat didn't reach, or it was poorly insulated, because it was just as chilly on a hot day when we were air conditioned, as a cold one when we were toasty with heat.

On more than one occasion, I had found drips on the stairs of something shiny, clear and sticky, like a transparent glitter glue. I would have been the only person in the library who might have been using a product like this, working with my children patrons, and I certainly hadn't dripped it down the stairs.

That was the only stair I knew of to reach the cellar room. I believe there also used to be another back stair to the cellar. This was behind a door in a storage closet in an upstairs staff office. I had been told that door had to remain clear for fire inspections, as it led to the furnace. But whenever we had to get to the basement, we used the freezing cold new staircase.

One more stair, on the western side of the house by the staff offices closed to the public, led up a half dozen or so steps to a wall. It had clearly been walled off so there was no longer any door or passage any further up. I assume there had been an attic at some point, now sealed off.

We had to take the new stairs to go down the cellar sometimes, to store book donations for a periodic used book sale. There were also equipment down there, the furnace, a computer server station, janitorial supplies used by the long-time custodian of the place. The cellar was ancient, like my Children's Room, with low beamed wood ceilings and of course many huge spiders.

On the nights I worked late, or in the winter when it was always dark by dinnertime, I sometimes noticed something peculiar once in my car. The chimney was glowing. It looked like a dusky orange light glowing from the chimney, reflected back down from the chimney cap. I don't know if a fire in a fireplace typically shows light visible from the outside, other than smoke. All I know is that the fireplaces in this library are not used. And that I didn't always observe this light at night, only occasionally, so if it was a reflection from the streetlamp, it selected its own occasions.

It wasn't until I had my own peculiar experiences in the library, and mentioned these to other staff, that I heard about the library's haunted reputation. It wasn't talked about publicly. I'm sure they didn't want to frighten patrons away, or open themselves to ridicule from skeptics.

But one night I asked my colleagues about the falling books and the smoke, and they gave me an earful of stories.

As I remember, no one else had sensed the smoke. I did hear then that a prior librarian had been a smoker, but not inside the library of course. But they absolutely believed that my story was otherworldly. They told me to tell them when I smelled it, but it never happened for them; it was always gone when I brought someone in to check.

They each had stories to share of being alarmed and frightened. One staff would absolutely not go into the basement. She would only say that she had had very creepy feelings there and had fled the room in mindless terror.

We had all had the experience of the exterior doors being randomly locked and unlocked. We would not be open yet, at work inside before hours, and specifically have checked to make sure the doors remained locked. And then someone of the public would come in, and we would find the door open. Or the reverse, throughout the day, during open hours: people may have been coming and going, and suddenly the doors were locked, and people were twisting the knob unable to get in.

The worst was at night, when there were only two staff present to close the library. This is when the staff had witnessed shared experiences. Two women who had worked there many years, remembered the time they had gone through the checklist, checking all the rooms, turning off all the lights, ready to alarm the place. I was told, "and then we heard women's voices upstairs! in the dark! coming from the poetry room, murmuring, and laughing! The hair on my arms stood up! We looked at each other and then actually ran out of here. We locked ourselves in our cars and drove off without looking back!

"I have never been so scared. Now we try to shut everything down upstairs while we still have people bustling about down here, while we have company, and noise. I don't like it when it's too quiet here. I don't want to just sit here by myself listening to the ghosts in this place."

?

What the--?

I F YOU'VE EVER BEEN to Bellingham, Washington, then you know it's got a certain magic about it. Some say it has a curse, that if you visit or settle down there, it's very hard to leave. And if you do you leave, you keep going back. Others say it's just weird. Well, as a long time resident and now a breaker of the curse, (I've finally moved away after three tries, though I still visit with caution), I can tell you it's still a little weird, but in a hipper way. Things change. But still, it's magical for sure, especially when the sun shines.

City center is set right on the edge of Bellingham Bay, where several islands of the San Juan archipelago jut up on the horizon, between northwest Washington State and Vancouver Island. Often, in late afternoon on "sunny" days, (which means clouds come and go), light bounces off the water so intensely as to be blinding. This is when the pubs and cafes that are lucky enough to have outdoor seating facing west, or west-ish, fill up quickly, even on chilly fall or spring days.

If you happen to be at the edge of town, you often have a view of Mt. Baker to the east. Its snowy volcanic peak rises up 10,000 and some odd feet. Stunning on sunny days. But even when it's veiled behind clouds, you can feel its immense presence. Like it's watching over, or protecting you.

The weirdness of Bellingham is hard to describe or understand. But you feel it. And you can tell other people must feel it too. It comes out in the way they dress. Anything goes, really. Striped mini skirts over flowery tights. Kilts and berets. Seattle Seahawk sweatshirts with wool socks and sandals. Lots of baggy shorts, year round; black trench coats from the thrift shop, and, of course, waterproof fabrics of all sorts of colors from muted greens to bright yellows. It rains a lot, (or at least it used to).

This "anything goes" way of being is also true for the kinds of people who live there, which is one of the reasons I loved living there. In the beer garden, hard core mountain bikers, covered in mud, sat with artists who sculpted with chicken wire, and classically trained musicians-turned-permaculture designers. Kayakers and climbers shared the open mic stages with poets, college students, and IT managers who played guitar and knew at least three songs. If you raised backyard chickens, you were cool,(as long as you didn't have a rooster). And if you happened to own your house, there was a good chance you would seriously consider painting it a shade of blue, red, or green that clashed with all the houses on your block.

When I was living there in the early 2000's, one summer night after a potluck in a friend's backyard, I drove home, a short drive across town. It was probably around ten o'clock or so by the time I parked my truck, scooped up my container of leftovers, and walked across the parking lot toward my apartment. It was a clear night, and despite the city lights, I could plainly see dozens of stars. When I reached the sidewalk to my building I looked up again into the sky. Honestly, I felt compelled to. About 45 degrees up and toward the north I saw the strangest thing. Three orange lights in the formation of a triangle moved slowly toward me. There was no sound. *Plane? Helicopter? No. What has three orange lights? But there's no sound? What the...?"*

Seconds passed and the three lights, still in a triangle, were right above me. I really don't know how far. Certainly not 50 or 200 feet. Much higher. But of course I didn't know the size of the thing that the lights were attached to. Or were they three separate things? The points of light seemed to be the size of big stars. If I had been a cartoon, my open jaw would have touched the ground with my eyes bulging out of my head!

Then, the triangle stopped moving. I was looking straight up at them now. A few seconds later, and poof! Each point of light flew out away from the others, keeping in line with their same geometry! They streaked across half the sky so fast and then they just disappeared!

I stood there in the quiet night in disbelief trying to digest the weirdness of it all. Lights on planes don't move apart.

On another evening in Bellingham, in the early 2000's or teens, I was walking home after seeing a friend's band play, and saw another set of lights. These too were orange. One by one they flew from up behind the Chuckanut Mountains to the south, in a perfect line that arced up over Bellingham Bay and then leveled out over the water, heading northwest. They were evenly spaced. (Note this was well before Starlink!) By the time I noticed them there were already three or four in sight. Then more. Five, six, seven. All in a line moving faster than a plane or helicopter, but not so fast that I couldn't count them. Twelve or thirteen in all.

Then they did the weirdest thing. One by one, starting with the first in line, they disappeared. Finally, the last one I saw come up from behind the mountain was the last orange light to disappear. It was as if they went behind a curtain. They all disappeared in the same place in the sky. Very weird.

If you ever get a chance, I highly recommend visiting Bellingham, Washington. For the magic and weirdness. Just be careful. You might be abducted by the curse!

?

Lornquin

I WAS RIDING MY bicycle one afternoon around the lowland west side of Lummi Island, something I did almost every day that one summer, to help me grieve the death of a good friend. Riding had always helped me process loss.

Lummi is a small island, just 24 square miles, a 12-minute ferry ride off the northwest corner of Washington State. There weren't as many hills on this loop, and the views were quite spectacular in every direction as the single lane road hugged the coastline. Other nearby islands of the San Juan Archipeligo rose up from Rosario Strait to the south and west. My favorite view was looking west toward Orcas Island and some of the Canadian Gulf Islands. I never remembered their names. The sky seemed enormous this day and the play of light off the clouds and water seemed otherworldly.

Too beautiful for my eyes, and certainly too beautiful for words. So I won't even try.

It was here along this stretch of road that I came upon an orange and black butterfly with two rows of white dots along his wings. He was sitting on the macadam a foot or so from the road's edge. Here tall grasses, pink fireweed, wild rose, and some bush I can't identify, which gives off one of the most intoxicating sweet aromas I've ever smelled, grew quite happily without threat from commercial mowers. It was still early summer before the roadside vegetation made its own threat of swallowing up civilization.

As I approached the little fella, I could see that one of his wings was torn, kind of like someone took a bite out of him. Poor guy. I figured he couldn't fly. Wanting to spare him a violent death by a rubber tire, I got off my bike, leaned it onto the grass, and knelt down to see him better. I was thinking I'd coax him onto my finger and move him under a bush where he would eventually have a more natural death, perhaps as a meal for one of his predators. That was just how life went for a butterfly. If you can't fly, you're not going to live that long.

This is when things got weird. Now I don't know how other people are with the critters and creatures of this world, but I talk to them. For me it's just a normal thing to do. I think most probably people do the same. I don't really know. Anyway, I introduced myself and told him I was sorry that he had an injured wing, and that I was going to move him out of the road so he wouldn't get squashed by a car. The little guy willingly walked onto my left index finger and stayed there, as I myself walked several yards off the road and leaned down to set him in the grass under a bush.

But he wouldn't leave my finger. I kept telling him that it was safer there under the bush, and that he was beautiful, and please jump off my finger. Still, he wouldn't go. In fact, he turned around and walked up my hand, and then my arm.

Now you can't be mad at a beautiful butterfly, but I was a little stern about my wanting to continue on with my bike ride, and how sorry I was, but he had to face his fate. I couldn't save him, just help him have a more natural butterfly death. He didn't listen. Or rather, he probably didn't understand a word I was saying. He just kept walking up my arm. Finally, he stopped on top of my left shoulder, inches from my chin as I stared into his little eyes.

Amused by this, I laughed out loud and repeated my intention to help him die a more dignified butterfly death. I stuck my right finger under his feet and asked him to please hop on so I could put him under the bush. He turned away and walked over my shoulder a little onto my back, still in view out of the corner of my eye. Now I was getting impatient.

"Okay, fine. Stay there if you like, but I'm going on my bike ride. You're welcome to come along, but it's going to be windy and you might end up far away from home." He just sat there.

Off I went. I thought for sure the little black and yellow butterfly with a bite out of his wing would soon jump off my back or be blown off by the force of air as I pedaled along. Every so often I'd turn my head as far as I could to see if he was still there. Every time he was. His wings fluttered in the steady breeze but his skinny legs and feet clung to my shirt. In disbelief I laughed in his face and continued to try to talk sense into him. "Like I said before, I'm going home. It's a few miles. You're welcome to come home with me, but then what? You can't fly. I'm sorry."

Half way home I started to feel obliged to do something for the little guy. But what? It was then that I made him a deal. "Okay, so if you want to come home with me, I promise I'll do what I can to give you a nice place to die." I thought for sure he wouldn't make it, especially when I reached a downhill section of road. There was just no way he could cling on.

He did.

When I got home, I carefully dismounted and leaned my bike against the garage. I looked over my shoulder at his tiny little wind-blown face and right into his eyes. "Congratulations, you made it! Amazing." He then walked up over my shoulder and down my left arm. I supposed he wanted something. So I pointed my right index finger under his front legs and he walked onto my finger. *Aha! He wants me to take him somewhere.* "Okay, buddy, here we go. There's a big field of high grass. You'll love it."

I walked to the edge of the field, knelt down, stretched my arm out into the grass and laid my hand on the ground, palm down. He wouldn't go. In fact, he turned around and walked back up my hand and arm. This was getting ridiculous. "Okay, okay. Fine. I'll take you inside, but inside is not like outside. You may not like it."

Once inside, it was clear I couldn't just put him in a chair or on the table. Surely I would accidentally sit on him or lose him in the clutter. So I took a little box from the recycling, went outside and gathered leaves and grass and a pine cone and made a home for him. Back inside, I set him down inside the box that sat next to the open window. I figured he might feel the breeze and feel more at home. He seemed content while I got a saucer for water and placed that in the middle of the box. There.

He didn't move much. I guessed he wasn't thirsty. Then I realized I didn't know anything about butterflies, so I opened my computer and got online. First I found out that he was a Lornquin's admiral butterfly. And then I learned that butterflies in general only live about 10 days. And that they taste with their feet. *Cool. And what did they like to eat?* Rotten fruit was a treat. *Yes! Perfect!* I still had a bowl of local cherries I'd picked two weeks earlier in the fridge that were definitely rotting. I proceeded to put the most rotten of them in a little bowl and placed that in the box too, next to his water. And that's when the party began!

My little friend slowly walked to the bowl of cherries and climbed on top of the heap. Now if I hadn't been fully awake and seeing with my very own eyes, I would have thought I was dreaming or on a magic mushroom trip. This beautiful little being took a few steps onto the rotting cherries with his tasting feet and began to dance! He lifted his head up and down and then whirled around and around like a dervish in a trance. Around and around he spun. "Oh. My. God." I laughed and cried and watched him dance, celebrating his incredible luck. A ride on a bike AND a bowl of rotting cherries!

When he stopped spinning, maybe four or five minutes later, (I'm not kidding), he steadied himself and got down to business. He stuck his long proboscis into a mashed cherry like a straw and proceeded to eat. And eat. He didn't move for a long, long time. "Be careful," I told him. "You're gonna get drunk!" I watched him for what seemed like an hour or more, gorging himself on the ferment of his last meal.

Soon, I, too, had to eat my own dinner, so left his side. Every so often I'd look in on him and, sure enough: still eating. Finally, after I'd finished my meal and puttered around cleaning up and catching up on emails and such, I noticed he had pulled out. He just sat there in a daze. Again, I laughed aloud. "Ha! See? You're drunk! I told you to be careful!"

I sat with him for as long as could before I fell into my own daze. Off to bed. *But wait. What if he climbs out of the box in his drunken stupor, falls on the floor where I step on him in the middle of the night if I get up?* Oh geez.

So, brilliantly, I took him out of the box and put him on the rug which happened to have had gold, brown, and black designs in the shape of butterflies. Not so brilliant. I'd lose him on the wool. Back in the box. Fortunately, he stayed put all night, thus avoiding the fate of my big bare feet.

By morning, I was thrilled to see him still in his box of leaves and grasses and pine cone, water dish and leftover rotten cherries. I looked again. He hadn't really moved too much since the night before. Maybe he was dead. Overdosed. I prodded him with a finger. Nope. He moved. Still alive! Whew! *Now what?*

Well, I couldn't think of anything else I could do. I supposed I could have taken him back outside under a bush in the high grass. But I didn't think he'd like that. He didn't before. Why would he now? He had food and water and no worry about predators. Besides, I'd grown fond of him. I moved his box closer to the window in hopes that he could feel the breeze under his wings. I know that might sound crazy to some people, but that's what you do, right? Well, it's what I did.

For the three days, Lornquin sat in his box on top of leaves and grasses next to his cherry bowl. He didn't walk around very much. Then he didn't walk at all. On the fourth day when I woke up and checked on him, he was still on his same perch and I just knew it. He was gone. His 10 days were up.

I lifted his weightless butterfly body out of the box and gently placed him on a beach stone set on my windowsill. He stayed there all summer with the breeze blowing over his drying wings. Come the following spring when I moved, I put him in a much tinier box all his own and wrapped that in bubble wrap.

Lornquin would move with me two more times until his frail little body finally broke apart. I don't remember what I did with him. At some point I probably thought I was being ridiculous for keeping him and threw his butterfly parts under a bush in the yard.

I loved that little fella.

?

I Heard the Creature of 7A

M Y PARENTS FELL IN love with Vermont, and took us there when we could go, for short vacations. We always took a route through Bennington up to Manchester where we often stayed, and then spent time in the surrounding villages, golf and ski resorts, at lakes and swimming holes. When we were grown, my sister and I each made our Vermont visits when we could, and my bride and I got married there on a Fourth of July.

As a result, we often vacation in the same area seasonally, but especially in the summer for our anniversary. There are so few people there, compared to our home, and so little traffic. Because the woods and mountains surround and encroach on human life there, we had sometimes encountered local wildlife such as moose. At home we have plenty of the kinds of wildlife which thrive in areas disturbed by humans, fox, coyote, raccoon, deer, even bear, and birds of course, owls, hawks and eagles. We also knew farm animals from the last of our local 4-H partner farms. All of these animals can make some pretty eerie sounds, especially in the middle of the night when you can't see them. Moose was a new acquaintance for us.

Then one Independence Day visit, we were in a motel-style road front lodging, woods behind, mountain views ahead, not much else. It was right on Historic Vermont Route 7A. Route 7A runs from Bennington through Manchester to Dorset. I stepped outside for a breath of air at around 11 P.M. My wife was in bed already.

There wasn't much to see in the utter darkness. Mere steps before me was the small parking lot, with one lonely light, then Route 7A, and across this road, darkness dropped off like a cliff into the ocean. It was pitch black.

Suddenly my heart dropped. I heard an excruciating call. It was some combination of a low, rumbling growl, grunts and a scream. It sounded like a very large animal; it had that deep barrel-chested reverberation. It was loud and sounded like it was right in front of me, like just barely outside the tiny pool of light from the lot. My wife heard it too and flew out. "What is that?" We stared at each other.

I rushed in to grab my video camera recording equipment and ran out again. I am a filmmaker and always carry my equipment to get extra scenic footage I might be able to use. My case was just inside the door on a desk. I told my wife I was headed down into that dark valley to shoot.

"What, are you crazy? That's what happens in horror movies! You'll never come back!" The sound was pretty terrifying. I turned on the camera as the roaring continued. I checked that it was recording; the meter was running. The call continued again, again. It kept repeating, splitting the air, for a long time. When the bizarre sound finally stopped for some time, we returned to bed.

I tried to review my recording. I had missed it! I had nothing. I couldn't understand. This would not happen to me. I always check and double check my tech. Somehow, the film had run and nothing of the sound was recorded.

I assumed it was a moose. I know they are huge animals and can make some very strange calls.

The next day when we told the owners about it at breakfast, they said they hadn't heard anything. They said they had never seen or heard a moose around there, though. We continued to ask around. When I described it, some people said it was likely a moose. Some said it was the Creature of 7A.

I will never forget this frightening sound. Of course I have been doing research on it ever since. Now, go and listen to all the recordings of moose sounds you can find. I have, and what we heard was not a moose. From what I can tell, all those moose recordings sound very much related to other cattle-like livestock. Not the same, but you could tell it was that kind of animal, similar; as loud and weird as it gets, it sounds like something in the cow family, to me. Listen to the varieties of bear. Close your eyes. They sound bear-like. They sound like what that kind of animal should sound like. Related to the dog family, even. At its most indistinguishable, a bear sounds like a huge predatory mammal. Think lion, but bear-ier.

I tell you, I've heard foxes, coyotes, eagles, bucks, moose even, at their absolute screechiest, snortiest and weirdest. This was nothing like that. It touched on hybrid-human sounding. Something vocal in it. It was obviously a call. If you were familiar with the tones, maybe a language or song, like bird calls have. I don't have the recording and I'm not good at describing it, or imitating the sound. We just know what we heard.

So I've continued my research. Are there Sasquatch observations in Vermont? Yes. Yes, there are. In fact, reportedly these date way back before all the hoax-y looking evidence common since I've been a kid. Now we are talking about the area I was in, that we frequent, in Southern Vermont. A series of sightings of a "gorilla man" in this area date all the way back to 1861. They formed posses to try to hunt it. It got away, described as almost supernatural in its evasion of them.

And then, way, way back, pre-USA. Local anthropologists say the First Vermonters, the original people here, told of a giant man, bear-like and human-like, hairy and cannibalistic. They describe its smells and its agility, its ability to disappear and elude in a fabulous manner.

Over the centuries many Vermonters, at home in the wilderness here and adept at wildlife spotting of moose and other native creatures, have reported seeing this giant hairy man creature, and noted how it escaped them so effortlessly.

People have also noted that one thing which distinguishes what they hear, from the strangest known moose calls, is the many, many repetitions of the call. The obviously huge size of the creature making the sound, explains why one would think, first, of Vermont's largest wild mammal, the moose.

I have no idea what made the sound I heard, but it was truly frightening in its strangeness and close proximity to me. I know I will never forget it.

?

The Bloody Kitchen

I LIVE IN A modern era suburban house, a bilevel. There is nothing less haunted-like than a bilevel, it has absolutely no character or history. Ours is very undistinguished. The house is on a small lot next to a row of others, on what used to be called, and still is on our street sign, a Dead End.

I have four to six children and an indeterminate number of cats. The numbers are a range because some aren't home, they're pretending to live in another family today; or my own have brought home some extras. Or, they have more kittens.

It was the summer vacation, not for me but for them. When I am away for work, even though most of them are old enough to stay alone--well not really, but the oldest is old enough--I instill a local young teenager to remain present and vigilant, and I pay her handsomely, if she is still there when I return home. And if this teenager happens to be my oldest, and if she is still there when I return, I pay her just as well. I do find that while any one of them is probably responsible enough to stay alone for a little while, adding children does not make them more responsible, only less. Fights break out between them, sometimes vicious. Sometimes they dare each other or try to top each other with risky adventures. Hence the need for an older child as guard.

The nice thing about the bilevel is that as distinct from everyone's standard finished beige carpeted basement, where most people store their children, as a bilevel this one actually has an emergency exit, and is not exclusively an underground firetrap with a tiny window you could only pass a baby through. So yes, the kids play and watch TV and eat down there, down the stairs from the kitchen, and can even sleep down there when necessary. And I can feel secure about it because it is part of the Living Space; we call it the Rec Room. We leave open the door between it and the garage, for the cats.

We don't have a dog anymore. We had a little whitish mix of a dog who had suffered a little brain damage. She took to anxiously protecting us, her eyes boring into one's own with anxiety for us, having to keep one paw on us at all times, and unable to bear if any of us were in separate rooms and not together under her watch. Which was fine because it just meant that I didn't bother to clean up after dinner. I would bring the dinner downstairs and sit with the kids all night in front of the TV in our rec room, to keep the dog content.

She wasn't content; she still anxiously guarded the patio door and barked at herself or something outside all night, but we could draw the drapes closed and she would settle until we all of us went up to bed, where she guarded me by staring at me all night and panting. Maybe it was the cats who made her anxious, but we closed the doors against them in the bedrooms, due to allergies. And to increase everyone's chances of survival in a fire.

At some point she couldn't bear guarding us anymore and we couldn't bear it either, and she heroically chased something out the kitchen, down the stairs, through the garage and squeezed out under the garage door and across the road and was murdered by a truck. She looks like an opossum at night ,and the driver didn't even stop to think it was someone's family.

We still had to draw the drapes at night because we fancied seeing her looking in at the patio door with her intensely anxious eyes, vigilantly counting the hairs on our heads and our eyelashes. We wondered if her reflection had been burned into the glass door somehow all those years.

Anyway this summer, we didn't have a dog anymore, other than that memory at the window.

I hired the sitter. So far the kids hadn't gone anywhere, all six or so of 'em, and the cats had stayed home and stayed inside because it was so darn hot out. The children weren't very energetic even in the morning when they got up all sweaty, so on this particular day they were planning to stay in the cool darkness downstairs and do their summer reading, (or play video games, I am no fool). I leave sandwich fixings in the fridge for them, and ice cream.

Well there was some storm that day, wouldn't you know, good thing they hadn't gone to the pool! When I got home the power was still out. When I went to put the key in the door I noticed it turned too easily, and I locked it instead of unlocking it. The door had not actually been locked. I irritably made note of this in my head, to yell about later.

Inside the door, a note was taped to the mirror, "Sorry Mrs. T.--had to go home. 2:00. Cathy". I muttered, but removed a bunch of bills out of the envelope with her name on it, and left the remainder on the table under the mirror.

There was a terrible smell in the kitchen, like rot, which I assumed was the fridge leaking. The power must have been out all day. The lights were out of course but being summer, there was still some light coming in the window. Enough to show the massacre that had taken place in that kitchen.

Roughly sliced pickles spilled off a plate, and a bloody knife was on the floor, and there was blood tracked everywhere. I didn't see any bandages, but there were bloody paper towels crumpled on the counters and a bloody kitchen towel dropped on the floor. Well, they've gone and done it, I thought. They've gone and killed each other. I screamed out some names. The door to the stairs was closed and a cat was scratching on the other side. The bloody tracks went to the door downstairs, and nowhere else.

Among the tracks were bloody paw prints of a dog. In my mind I heard a dog's whining, but I think it was just the buzzing in my ears from panic.

I stepped down the stairs fearful for what I would find. Sure enough, all those kids of mine, and guests, lay tumbled on the floor, with blood-matted hair, or blood-smeared shirts, and spots on the upholstery.

Just then the power flashed on, and the TV flashed back on with some loud blare of ridiculousness. And a dog, somewhere, was barking. And the kids started moving, sitting up on their elbows, squinting at me in the light. And I could see there were little military people game pieces scattered everywhere, and greasy paper plates with half eaten burgers on top of a game board on the table. And the blood caked in my children's hair was, on closer look, just ketchup.

"We made burgers!"

I was too weak with relief to scream at them. Good thing the meat didn't go to waste in the outage. I sank into the sofa and pushed the children off to go and wash themselves. I couldn't face returning to the kitchen just yet to clean out the refrigerator and mop up the ketchup explosion and pawprints.

Dog prints?

A car's headlights flashed in as someone turned around in our dead end. The sliding glass door flashed an apparition of a little doggy face looking in at us, laughing at me.

?

Something Was There

N O ONE LIVED IN our house before us. It was new construction when my family moved in when I was two years old. If you live in a house built just before you moved in as the first occupants, don't you feel pretty confident it isn't haunted?

Nothing bad has happened here yet. No one died here, because no one has ever lived here before.

Before our house was built, the lot was part of a small farm. The farmer subdivided and used a small builder to build just a half dozen houses, in a row, on the road. My parents thought the original owner or builder scooped up the topsoil and took it with them, and left us with sterile clay. Now that I've learned more about conservation of soil in our area, I doubt that was true. Our part of the country is a lot of clay, and the land was farmed for a long time. There are native cedars sprung up here, and our street is named for them. There are woods behind, a row of undeveloped lots, with only a paper street on the town map.

Before the farms, I suppose it was originally land inhabited by indigenous peoples. Over the years, we've found arrowheads. We've also dug up old farm-type implements, parts of tools, knives, unknown rusty things. A vintage bow hunting quiver tool.

We grew up here, never afraid. Of course the usual childhood nighttime fears, calling dad in to check for a cricket chirping somewhere. Mild stuff. My little brother slept across the hall, with all his stuffed animals. A sturdy, safe, peaceful house, the heat blowing on when the chilly morning dawned. A faithful train whistle meant the commuters' day had begun. And at nighttime, the reassuring background noise of a television away downstairs marking my parents' wakefulness.

Maybe I had the occasional nightmare of a man from the woods breaking into the kitchen.

I was a sleepwalker. My parents were frightened that I would fall down the stairs, because sometimes I walked dragging blankets with me. I do not remember these episodes. I outgrew it.

As a teen I experienced my first death in the family. My grandmother died, way too young, and suddenly. My grandmother and mother had both been young parents, so she was not like an old person. She was close to us and we were shocked. At first I was sure it wasn't true, and that she'd been buried alive. My mother's grief was severe.

I got back into my school routines, somewhat changed by this new experience of loss. I ended a dating relationship with someone I suddenly realized I didn't like much. I let go a few casual friendships.

Months later, I was sleeping contentedly in my serene room, my cozy house, when I started to notice some strange changes. A clock I had on the wall would suddenly start ticking really loudly, echoing. I complained to my parents. My father stuffed cotton batting into the back of the clock. But still, only sometimes, it would tick really loudly, even wake me. And then sometimes when this happened, the rocking chair in my room rocked. I didn't feel afraid by these things though. I thought it could be my grandmother visiting. I didn't feel threatened, only the noisy clock disturbed my sleep. We got rid of the clock.

It's strange how you don't feel frightened during a ghost's visit. Some people go looking for ghosts. I never wanted to be visited, ever. I never wanted anything strange to happen because I thought it would be like the movies, too scary. But I didn't feel afraid.

Until late one night, I was in bed, sleepy but not asleep yet. The rest of the house was silent and asleep. I heard steps in the hallway creaking up the stairs in order, as they might if someone were walking up them. At the top, I heard no more footsteps in the hallway. Then I heard a scratching on my door, about two feet from the floor. We had no pets. Scratch, scratch, scratch, like claws. I have since heard many mice in walls and squirrels on the roof and this was nothing like that scritching, scrabbling, chewing. The doors on the rooms were those light, hollow wood veneer interior doors. The noise distinctly came from that spot low on the outside of the door, scratching, clawing.

I went cold with fear.

I just listened. It stopped.

I was a good student, read a lot. I read big books in bed late at night, I stayed up writing papers. I became loathe to turn off the lights. I don't know if my mind was overworked, having stayed up too late with reading and homework, but tired as I was, I just didn't want to sleep. And I became a little fearful about getting out of bed to cross the room to turn off the light. The light only made things worse though. I am very nearsighted, so things can appear strange without glasses, especially in dim light. I felt like the darkness might have been comforting, but I kept that light on. I am not sure why.

In some classes my grades slipped a little because I was tired. Mostly I made it through and ultimately learned to distract myself, so I was able to go off to college and there, to sleep at night.

Only once have I been frightened since arriving home again. One afternoon when no one else was here, I heard the distinct sounds of someone walking and knocking about upstairs. I was frightened enough to get on the phone with someone for company. I was so scared that I wanted to leave the house, but there was police activity outside on the street. Was there a criminal on the loose? Was he in the house? The sounds stopped as soon as I connected on the phone.

I wouldn't think anything of my experiences, except for this. I still live in this house, and raised my children here. And my grown daughter, knowing nothing about my own tale, said she had had a situation in this house, as a teen. She had a story of her own to tell. But then she was never able to share it. She said she couldn't bear to think about it. I know only that she believed she had witnessed a demon upstairs. We had reconfigured the bedrooms somewhat, made three rooms from two. And in the room which was where mine would have been, she had been terrorized by what she called a demon.

Then she went off to school, and eventually returned home.

We continue to occupy these rooms without incident, except for the mice. Whatever it was seems to have just passed through and gone, because the house has been nothing but serene and peaceful since, guarded only by our own sweet family spirits and happy memories. I feel so safe and content here.

But what my daughter and I both remembered from those old days, was something very frightening that accompanied us at the same place and point in our life. Does this happen to everyone, or is it just present here in this place, waiting?

?
Poltergeists

I DON'T REALLY BELIEVE in supernatural explanations for when weird things happen. I usually assume there must be some rational reason, I just don't know it yet.

Like every now and then, someone knocks at the door in the early morning, when it is still dark. I know it's no neighbor or passerby or stranger in need. There's never anyone there. We live in a semi-rural area. No one walks across wide open acreage to bang on my door. I know all the woodpeckers in the neighborhood, and the different sounds of their work on the trees or even on the gutters. This is a couple knocks at the door, which as suddenly stop. I note it, it doesn't bother me.

But this time there was a regular series of weird things that happened all together, every day in a week. Maybe it's just the stuff that happens all the time, coincidences, and for some reason this time I noticed them. You tell me.

We were just getting to the very darkest days in the year, after daylight savings time ended, just about the winter holidays when night sets in before five o'clock.

I have an old dog, and she is going blind, and has arthritis, and is disoriented at night. So I have to sleep on the floor in the living room with her these days, just so I can actually get some sleep myself. The vet suggested she needs a nightlight in the dark, because her vision is so poor, so I leave the television on for light and white noise.

One night, when I was putting away the dinner leftovers, there wasn't enough room to fit the last scoop of kale into the storage bowl. So I put it into a small bowl to finish it off as a bedtime snack. I know, I shouldn't eat at night, but I was too lazy to find storage for just this scoop, and too guilty about throwing it away. It was just kale, (and garlic and stuff) and it had been really good. So I ate it, in the living room, in front of the TV. I put the empty bowl, with the fork in it, on top the tea table in there, which has a small tablecloth on it.

I sleep on a folding mattress. When I set it up, I push this swiveling tea table out of the way. My dog and I retired to the mattress, but I sat up working on my laptop for awhile.

When I got sleepy, I reached up and put my laptop on top the table. I didn't want it to fall off the table, so I pushed it well onto the table so it wasn't near the edge. It was on the tablecloth, the tablecloth hung evenly all four corners around the table, so all seemed good. The table is not exactly right next to my mattress. Between me and the table, I have a bin of dog treats, and a little basket with my TV remote, dog pills, glasses, cell phone, etc. The fall-asleep programming on the television always stays on all night until morning; we went to sleep.

At four a.m., I woke to a crash. Oh no! My laptop was flat on the floor, upside down, next to me! It had fallen off the table! I was so distressed about whether that laptop was broken! And still falling, were the ceramic coasters which were on the table, and then the tablecloth slid off the table on top of everything!

The dog was asleep next to me.

And it was dark, but for a nightlight across the room and in the kitchen; the TV was off, somehow. It always stayed on all night. Was there a power outage? No, none of the clocks or devices were blinking with a power failure notice. I had to find the remote to put it back on, for light.

I couldn't find the black thing in the dark, so I had to get up and put on the lights.

Get this. The table was bare of the tablecloth, but my bowl, and one coaster, were still on the table! Even though I had carefully placed it on the tablecloth, which was now on the floor.

Now you may tell me, there's a magic trick for snatching a tablecloth really fast, from a certain angle, leaving dishes on the table. But you tell me: who was the magician?

The bowl was there, but the fork was missing. I looked around, I couldn't find the fork. I figured I'd see it in the morning.

When I folded up the mattress when the sun had risen, there was a spoon, not a fork, and it was under the mattress.

Oddities continued daily after this. Well, speaking of odd, I have to confess more peculiarities of my lifestyle. Really it's just because I am a practical person.

I get dressed down the cellar. The washer and dryer are there, and I am a busy person. I grew tired of carrying loads of clean clothes up two flights of stairs to put away up there, where I'm not even sleeping, and then hauling them back down to be washed, again and again. I don't mind the stair climbing, it's just the wasted time and work which bothers me. So now I have a few plastic drawers and a clothesline down there, and after washing them I stowe my clothes in the drawers or hang them on the line. I get dressed down there in the morning, and change for bed down there, where I can just throw my clothes directly in the wash.

So over the next week after the tablecloth trick, I went down to get dressed. Now, I say I put the clean clothes right away, but I've been kind of busy, so I do have some clean piles in baskets right now. And I have bins of holiday decorations stacked here and there too, because it's that time of year and I've been rummaging. So there's one nice clean pathway to walk on to my little stool by the washer where I sit and get dressed.

And this week, this happened. The first day, I look down, and right before my feet on the floor, I see my mother's funeral prayer card. We used a variety of them because I couldn't pick just one. This was one from a series with artwork from Russian icons, this was Jesus and on the reverse was the St. Francis prayer for peace. "Lord, make me an instrument of your peace: where there is hatred, let me sow love; where there is injury, pardon...", and maybe you know the rest.

Well I thought, hmm, no idea where that was, but it must have fluttered down here from some box or pile. I looked around a little and couldn't find the source. I picked up the card and brought it upstairs.

The next morning, I was getting dressed down there. I look down. There's another card, same prayer, slightly different Russian-style icon, the Virgin Mary and Infant Jesus. I marvel at this, and bring it upstairs to my desk.

The third morning, there is a third card, in the same empty spot the two prior had been. Same prayer, a different icon of Jesus. I bring it upstairs to my desk. I contacted my cousin to wonder about these "signs". Of course I feel there has to be a rational reason how I found one a day for three days in a row in the same spot. But it's starting to feel like a message, right?

The same evening as my communication with my cousin about this, right afterward I went down there to get changed for bed. I find, in the same place, a funeral prayer card. This one has the Hail Mary prayer on the back, and an image of Mary appearing as the Immaculate Conception.

Now I really hate to bring these religious items into the story because I don't like to profane them with joking talk about ghosts and poltergeists. I wouldn't want to offend. I don't like to think of the saints as restive spirits, and maybe whoever puts the cards there for me can't even read them. The context may only be mine, and I can certainly benefit from an urging to pray for peace, with instructions how to bring peace into the world, myself. I am just telling you what I found, and where, and how. I can't figure out how they got there, any more than I can, the tablecloth situation.

The very next night, this happened. And now I'm scared. Because this is too many odd things in a row. Again, with the food at bedtime: my dog's dinner plate is on the floor in the kitchen next to the water bowl. I keep the water bowl right where the light falls across the corner of the refrigerator, so that the water will reflect and she can find it. The plate is about six inches diameter. I serve her cooked chicken or turkey, or boiled eggs. She doesn't always eat anymore, and I often have to throw it away. I especially don't want to leave food out at night in case of mice.

But on this particular night, I left it out for awhile. I thought she might be hungry, and eat some on her next kitchen trip. I thought she would sleep better if she ate something.

When I got up in the wee hours myself, as I do, the dog was asleep. I walked into the kitchen to start coffee. I don't know why it scared me so, but when I saw this, I froze in fear and dread.

The dog's plate was pushed into the middle of the passageway. Smack into the center of my path to the kitchen. Like the cards had been in the center of the path at my feet, down the cellar. All the food was still there. I knew the dog hadn't pushed it. In the thirteen years she has been with us, she has never moved the plate.

That has to be some pretty big mouse, to move that plate.

I checked the time. It was 4:40 a.m. I threw away the food and put the dish in to be washed.

I am afraid now. I dread the next surprise. I can't wait to open the door to let the sun in, when it rises.

?

A Light in the Darkness

MY MOTHER LOVED CHRISTMAS!

She had always had the Christmas Eve table sparkling in candlelight and fairy lights glowing among the tableware, flashes of light from the table at the center of a room in complete darkness, for the hush of Christmas Eve, waiting.

The year she died, she had been planning Christmas for many months. She purchased a new lace tablecloth for the dining room table, which reminded her of her grandmother's Ukrainian table, with the hay underneath it to celebrate the Christ child's birth in the manger. She said this year we were going to have Christmas everywhere! Of course she usually did have marks of Christmas in every room of the house. It sounded like she was planning something even more extraordinary.

She died in November, in the month of death for so many. She died on the 14th, the date her mother died.

She was cremated, many miles from home. Three days after her death, our own backyard miraculously smelled–in cold November–like a combination of roses and buttered burnt toast.

In our grief, I figured on a more somber Christmas. Mother had carefully laid away the new tablecloth, in a dresser drawer scented with a woody musky sachet. It almost smelled like fresh hay in that drawer. I would use the tablecloth. I didn't know what her other Christmas plans had been, but I would decorate with serene wintry items, not too jolly or funny, because we were feeling so low in our mourning.

Meanwhile my father went to the cellar and brought up every last holiday item, every ho-ho-ho, every childish Santa, and grimly set them about the house. I am sure he felt he was fulfilling her intention, and his duty to carry on, caring for the rest of us.

We made it through with bottomless pots of coffee and daily visits from my brother, a habit we continue today more than ten years later. Our open wound healed over where the branch of our tree was lost, but we bear the scar, of course.

The roses I'd given her the day before she died, to apologize for some cruel and thoughtless daughter's remark I'd made, stayed fresh and unmarred for nearly a year. Eventually I removed the petals for potpourri, and they were still unusually fragrant, more than ten years later. I keep them shut in the china cabinet and they waft out like incense around the tabernacle when we open the door to set some holiday table.

On the twelfth year, I donated to our church to light a memorial Christmas tree in the church dooryard, in the name of "my mother who loved Christmas". The placard was misspelled: "for my mother who lived Christmas," but that was just as true.

Now our dog tends to be sick and unsettled at holidays. No, she never eats anything not meant for her, and we don't have chocolate. I figured she is aware of my attention to something else I am thinking about and feels anxious about it, or perhaps she lives in dread of having to bark at visitors, though we never have any other than the family she sees daily. Maybe she dreads the next package delivery person on the doorstep.

On the first Easter after my mother's death, the dog had barked and barked and barked at some point high over the corner she had once sat in, on precisely the cardinal western point of the house. I assumed it was some reflection or shadow, or spiderweb or who knows, though my father carefully noted it for memory. Being a scientist, he often captures and records data for assessment, over time, of some theory.

This barking habit would happen periodically on holidays over the years. Sometimes the dog followed the barking with scratching at the floor, behind the chair in this western corner, trying to dig a hole it seemed.

Might it be true, as many cultures believe, that West is the doorway to the next world, to the Divine? Is someone there at the door?

Well now, thirteen years since our loss, I was preparing for Easter celebration. We didn't all get new clothes this year for Easter as is traditional, but I did find an oilcloth white lace tablecloth for the kitchen table. I had a memory of a tablecloth like it on my great-grandmother's kitchen table; it was oilcloth for wiping clean, suitable for the work table. I was very pleased with mine and feeling comforted in my nostalgia. Easter is the holiday I most associate with my mother's Ukrainian mother and grandmother. I remember taking the basket of food to be blessed, in the dark, with a little lighted candle in each basket.

It was in April, a week or two before Easter, in the middle of the night, and I was sitting up in that chair in the western corner of the living room, holding the dog. She hadn't been sleeping through the night and wanted to be held, and this was the most comfortable recliner in which to relax as a substitute for sleep. I sometimes scroll through my phone, with her in my lap, until I can doze off again.

The dog startled, and my attention was drawn across the room. It was a dark, windy night, well after midnight. No cars were on the road, and there is no street light in front of our house.

In front of the window, on the windowsill behind the loveseat, I saw the sparkling colorful lights of a tiny Christmas tree, twinkling on and off all over, just like a real tree with fairy lights would look.

No Christmas decorations were still in the living room of course! We were preparing for Easter. I stared and stared and tried to assess what was causing my optical illusion. I saw no source for the light, and it continued for many minutes. I wasn't asleep; I even picked up my phone and recorded video of this phenomenon, which has alarmed all of my family when I show it to them. What was making the twinkling of lights in the shape of a tiny Christmas tree? No lights were on in the room. I watched it for many minutes. While I was watching, it eventually subsided.

I have watched the windowsill for many nights since, but nothing has appeared.

But a few weeks later, on Easter, this same thirteenth year, these things happened. After dinner, in the evening, the dog likes to play fetch with a toy. We played for some time and then she settled into a nap, and finally my father went to bed. His room is next door to this one.

I remained for a few minutes on the loveseat across the room. Suddenly the dog got up and brought her toy over to that chair. She held it up and sought someone or something high above the chair, whining for someone invisible to throw her toy. It was just as she would whine for one of us to throw the toy, but she was playing with an empty chair! I called my father to come and see this. We both stood across the room calling to her, "We are over here! There's no one there!" She persisted in crying to play with the empty space above the chair.

We also noticed that the ends of a very old folk-embroidered tablecloth over the tea table, next to the chair, were trembling as if in a breeze. I pointed this out, and we agreed that there was no breeze; the air conditioning was not on, the heat had been turned off, the windows were closed.

Finally when I moved to go get my phone to capture the dog's strange conduct, she stopped crying, looked around at the two of us, and stood there looking completely confused.

My father went back to bed, and the dog and I resumed our nightly routine.

I told my brother the story the next morning. My father added, "But there's more.

"After I went back to bed, I lay there reading for awhile, as always. Suddenly I felt someone stroking my hair on top of my head. I lay perfectly still paying attention to this feeling. When it stopped, I gingerly held my hand just above my head where I had felt the stroking, and my hair was electrified–my hair stood up on end to touch my hand.

"I fell asleep wondering about this, and woke sometime later, questioning, 'could this have been a visit from my wife?' I looked up at the digital clock display on the ceiling: It read '4:44'."

My father is convinced this special number was an angelic message.

For a few days to follow, the dog continued to entertain someone invisible whenever we were together. When we were all seated in the living room occupying the other chairs, she brought her toy over to an empty chair, one no one usually sat in, and whined directly to no one for the toy to be thrown.

When we were outside in the garden, she brought her toy to the empty Appalachian rocker. I watched her repeatedly bringing her toy to the empty chair. And it wasn't just the dog this time; I noticed that the chair was rocking to and fro slightly, though the identical rocker right next to that one was still. Now that rocker was really hard to get rocking, even when you're sitting in it and trying to rock. The pair of chairs are on an unevenly bricked patio. It really takes some leg muscle to get it moving, which is what I like about them, a little exercise while shooting the breeze. No moving air was perceptible, and the rockers are slatted all over, there isn't a solid surface to interrupt wind. I'd never seen either of them rock in the wind.. But surely it must have been a breeze?

The dog seems to have returned to herself since then.

I am sure this all sounds silly as it is only small strange things which occurred. But perhaps it's attention to small things which maintain our connection. Maybe a lingering or passing memory is the sparkle of light for a moment in our darkness.

? My Childhood Orbs

WHEN I WAS A little girl, maybe seven or eight, I slept in a little bed, with a white headboard, under soft cotton white sheets and a heavy wool blanket. My parents set my bedtime at 8 o'clock, even though lots of times I wasn't all that tired yet. Sometimes I would listen to my radio, especially when *Only The Shadow Knows* was on. I didn't mind just lying there staring up at the ceiling, because I loved to let my mind wander. And wonder, too. If the moonlight poured through the window, I wondered about shadows and angles. If it was raining, I wondered how long it took a raindrop to trickle down the roof, into the gutter, and down the spout into the flower bed. If I heard an owl outside, I wondered if it was saying goodnight to all of its owl friends. Eventually, my wandering thoughts and all my wondering got mixed up weird and I would fall asleep without ever knowing when or how that happened.

Now I never was really afraid of too much then. Well, except for the dark woods in the back. See, my father was big and strong, and loved me very much. I knew he would always protect me from scary things. And my mother was strong, too, in her own way, even though she was a tiny woman.

So when I lying in bed waiting to fall asleep, and the balls of soft light came, and floated around in my room, I wasn't afraid at all. And of course I wondered about them. They came about ten times or so that one summer and fall. They were the size of tennis balls and just floated all around the room. I knew they weren't headlights from passing cars because I knew what those looked like. Though these did move across the ceiling and wall, sort of like headlights, I'd seen headlights and those were straight beams. These were round, not flat round, but distinct spheres.

Sometimes there were three to six at once, all floating around so smoothly, up and down in arcs and swoops, and never a sound. I kept trying to listen harder, but there was no sound. Most times they stayed for five minutes or so, I think. Once or twice, I fell asleep before they left, but when I did see them leave, they would disappear one by one, like their bulb just flicked off.

It wasn't until I was an adult and heard other stories about people seeing orbs of light, that I started to think more about them. Then, when I saw a program on television that showed people's photographs of them, I instantly recognized the balls of light. Since then, I've wondered a lot about them. Lots of people see them. Outside in nature, and inside old houses and new. Are they some kind of being, like a big round firefly that always has its light on? Are they spiritual guides? I know that children of that age are supposedly more aware of the spiritual realm.

When I told my mother about them, she said they were just car lights.

But she didn't see them.

The world is full of strange and wonderful things, and the more I learn about it, the more I realize how little I know.

Bram Stoker

?

Notes, and for
Further Research

Manhattan Smith

- This tale is a retelling based on Michael Wojik's account in G.O.S.tV Episode One, "The Great Train Wreck", of Brian Vadim's and Jennie Collucci's video series on YouTube. The story is included in this collection with permission of Brian Vadim.

- Photographs of the Wreck of the Oswego Express, October 4, 1877, from the Milford Borough Historical Society:

The Wreck of the Oswego Express, October 4, 1877

https://milfordnjhistorica.wixsite.com/milford-nj-hist ory [Accessed December 16, 2023.]

- Find more vintage photographs and other historic resources at the West Jersey History Project. https://westjerseyhistory.org/images/hunterdon /milford/ [Accessed December 16, 2023.]

Old Dutch

- This tale is a retelling based on the accounts and reenactments in the film *The Ghosts of Somerville: Old Dutch Parsonage* from Brian Vadim, used with his permission. See where to stream: IMDB.https://www.imdb.com/title/tt1550317 0/ [Accessed December 16, 2023.]

- Learn more about the history of the New Jersey State Historic Sites, Wallace House and

Old Dutch Parsonage, by visiting the sites with a guided tour by an expert historian.

* Read about the sites: New Jersey State Park Service https://www.nj.gov/dep/parksandforests/histori c/wallacedutch.html,

* and *see* *also* the Wallace House and Old Dutch Parsonage Association. http://www.wallacehouseassociation.org/

Haunted Library

* This tale is set in the Raritan Public Library. Learn about the building's history and architecture at https://raritanlibrary.org/history[accessed December 16, 2023].

* For a fictional story inspired by this library and other local history, but entirely a product of the author's imagination, read: Seas, June. *The Look of Things: Mystery of the Haunted Library,* Carolingian Press 2022. This novel is part of *The Freep Investigates Mysteries Series* for young readers.

I Heard the Creature of 7A

- For the excellent summary of the history of "Bigfoot" sightings in Vermont, referenced in "I Heard the Creature of 7A", *see* Bartholomew, Robert and Pluta, Michael, "Bigfoot—Man, Myth or Monster?", Rutland Herald, [Accessed December 15, 2023.]

- *See* Map of Historic 7A. *OpenStreetMap, https://www.openstreetmap.org/copyright*[Accessed December 16, 2023.]

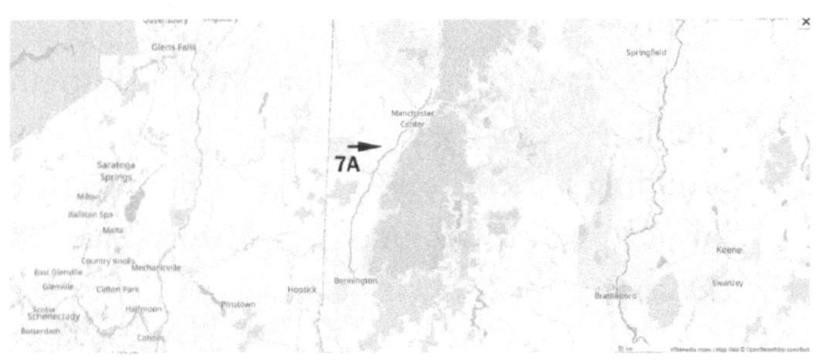

- For more information on taking Historic Route 7A in Vermont, try Aiken, Ken: "Riding Vermont Historic Route 7A", Rider Magazine, 2014;or Aiken, Ken: "A Trip Back in Time: Touring Vermont's Historic Route 7A", TouringRoads Travel & Adventure.[Accessed December 16, 2023.]

Poltergeists

- According to Encyclopedia Britannica, "'Poltergeist', (from German *Polter,* 'noise' or 'racket'; *Geist,* 'spirit), in occultism, [is] a disembodied spirit or supernatural force credited with certain malicious or disturbing phenomena, such as inexplicable noises, sudden wild movements, or breakage of household items...Such events are said to be sporadic, unpredictable, and often repetitive...According to popular belief, a poltergeist's activity appears to concentrate on a particular member of a family, often an adolescent..." *Britannica,* 2023. https://www.britannica.com/topic/poltergeist-occultism [Accessed December 16, 2023.]

- However, some paranormal scientists believe that "poltergeist" phenomena may be psychokinetic activity caused by a living human. For example, see the discussion by Jennie Collucci, Paranormal Investigator at Parasight Experience, in the film *Ghosts of Somerville: Old Dutch Parsonage.* Find where to stream the film for free on IMDB. https://www.imdb.com/title/tt15503170/ [Accessed December 16, 2023.]

- And some think the phenomena has other,

ordinary, physical and mechanical causes.

The remaining tales in this collection were shared with the authors by acknowledged individuals. We don't publicly share their identities or locations, to maintain their personal privacy.

Find More Stories

S. L. Vadimsky is the performer of these audiobooks.
Learn more at Carolingian Press Books.
True Tales of Ghosts
More True Tales of Ghosts and Weird Encounters
Sam 527
Games to Play with Your Sasquatch Friends
Snakeskins and Signposts
Legendary Fairy Tales
Nutcracker Rich
The Good Queen's Daughter
C. L. Vadimsky writes short stories, and writes young people's literature as **June Seas**. Look for these:
True Tales of Ghosts
The Look of Things: Mystery of the Haunted Library, by June Seas
"Gray Area" in *Tales From the Monoverse, a Last Waltz Anthology*

Sally Girl, A Slightly Scary Short Story
and more!
If you would like to hear more ghost stories on other media, check out the movies and and video serials from **Brian Vadim** exploring some of the stories in this book. *The Ghosts of Somerville: Old Dutch Parsonage* on IMDB *G.O.S. tV: The Great Train Wreck*on YouTube

Sign up on our website Carolingian Press Books for occasional email news and get a free short story, updates and deals;, or contact us through the website.
If you would like to hear more ghost stories on other media, check out the movies and and video serials from **Brian Vadim** exploring some of the stories in this book. *The Ghosts of Somerville: Old Dutch Parsonage* (link to IMDB for where to watch)
*G.O.S. tV: The Great Train Wreck*on YouTube
And view *The Ghosts of Somerville: Mrs. Micks,* (link to IMDB for where to watch), for discussion and reenactments of the "Mrs. Micks" tale in the book *True Tales of Ghosts.*

About the Authors

Salt and Pepper are cousins. They named themselves Salt 'n' Pepper when they were growing up. Together they added spice to the family's invented games. All the cousins loved music and physical feats and jokes and campfire tales. There were many storytellers over generations in their family, and they listened and soaked up the stories.

Now that Salt and Pepper are grown, they love to investigate and share the weird and wild truths that captivated them as kids. One lives on the East Coast and one on the West Coast, but they still get together. In spirit.

Salt

Songwriter, author, narrator, S. L. Vadimsky is inspired by nature, adventure, simplicity, conversation, and relationship. S.L. started life on a wooded lot in New Jersey, grew up in rural Pennsylvania, migrated to the West Coast and has claimed Bellingham, Washington and Port Angeles, Washington as home, between cycling trips and extended stays across the country.

Pepper

C.L. Vadimsky of Somerville, New Jersey, educated in Boston, writes short stories such as "Gray Area" in *Tales From the Monoverse, a Last Waltz Anthology;* and *Sally Girl, A Slightly Scary Short Story.*

She also writes as June Seas for young readers.